A+ books
BILINGÜE/BILINGUAL

Mídelo
Measure It

¿Cómo mides los
líquidos?

How Do You Measure
Liquids?

por/by Thomas K. & Heather Adamson

CAPSTONE PRESS
a capstone imprint

Tim and his mom are back from walking the dog. Everyone is thirsty.

Tim y su mamá regresaron de caminar al perro. Todos tienen sed.

Who has the most water?

¿Quién toma más agua?

2

Different shapes can make measuring liquid tricky.
Tim tries a ruler. The blue sport bottle is taller than the orange one. But rulers only show how tall or how deep something is.

Formas diferentes pueden dificultar la medición de líquidos. Tim prueba con una regla. La botella deportiva azul es más alta que la naranja. Pero las reglas sólo muestran qué alto o qué profundo algo es.

3

Tim needs to measure how much, or the amount of, liquid. He needs a container.

He fills the blue sport bottle all the way. Then he pours all the water into the orange bottle. But the orange bottle doesn't fill up.

The orange bottle is shorter, but it holds more.

Tim necesita medir cuánto, o la cantidad de, líquido. Él necesita un recipiente.

Él llena la botella azul hasta el borde. Luego, vierte toda el agua en la botella naranja. Pero la botella naranja no se llena totalmente.

La botella naranja es más baja pero contiene más.

Tim then fills up the orange bottle and pours it into the dog bowl. **Uh-oh.** The water doesn't fit. The dog bowl holds less water.

Tim luego llena la botella naranja y la vierte en el tazón del perro. **¡Oh, oh!** El agua no entra. El tazón del perro contiene menos agua.

Tim's orange bottle had the most water!

¡La botella naranja de Tim tiene la mayor cantidad de agua!

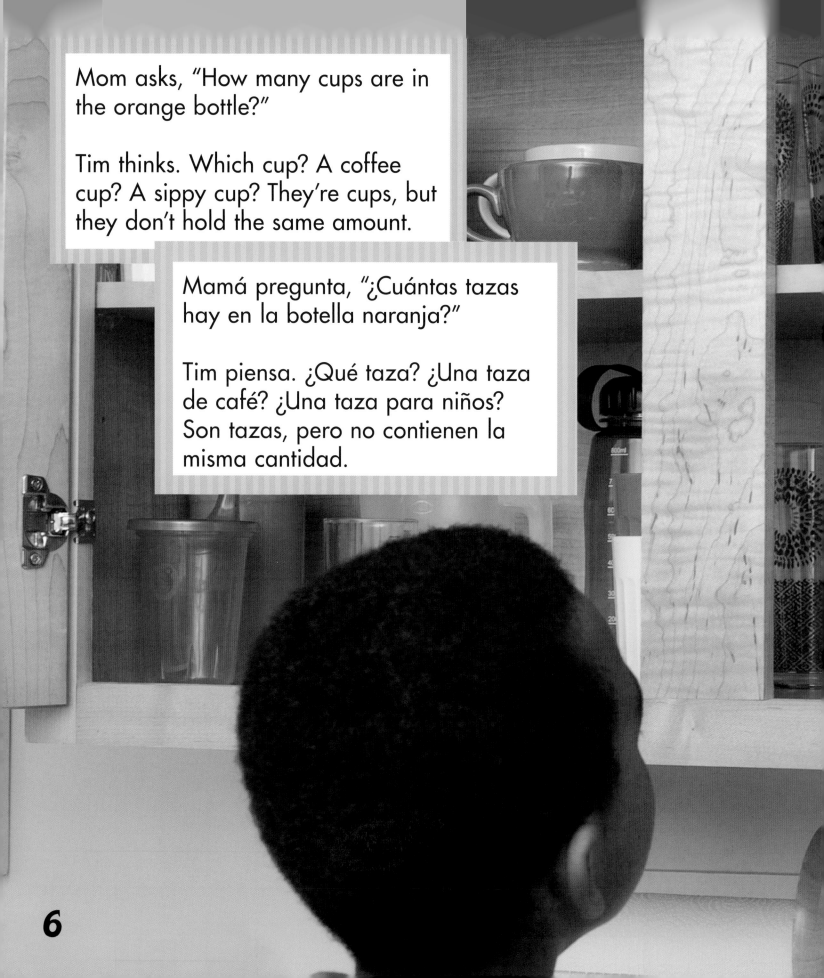

Mom asks, "How many cups are in the orange bottle?"

Tim thinks. Which cup? A coffee cup? A sippy cup? They're cups, but they don't hold the same amount.

Mamá pregunta, "¿Cuántas tazas hay en la botella naranja?"

Tim piensa. ¿Qué taza? ¿Una taza de café? ¿Una taza para niños? Son tazas, pero no contienen la misma cantidad.

7

Mom meant a measuring cup. People have made standard tools so everyone can measure the same way. Measuring spoons, cups, and pitchers have marks to show amounts of liquid.

Mamá quiso decir una taza medidora. La gente ha hecho herramientas estándar para que todos puedan medir de la misma manera. Las cucharas, las tazas y las jarras medidoras tienen marcas para mostrar cantidades de líquido.

We measure liquids by pouring them into the tool. Put the measuring container on a level spot. Get down low so your face is even with the container.

Nosotros medimos líquidos vertiéndolos dentro de la herramienta. Coloca el recipiente medidor en una superficie nivelada. Agáchate de manera que tu cara quede pareja con el recipiente.

Look at the lines on the side.

Mira las líneas de su lado.

9

People use cups, pints, quarts, or gallons to measure large amounts of liquid.

For smaller amounts, use teaspoons, tablespoons, and fluid ounces.

1 gallon/galón = 4 quarts/cuartos

½ gallon/galón = 2 quarts/cuartos

1 quart/cuarto = 2 pints/pintas

SELL BY
1% MILK
VITAMIN A&D • 1% MILKFAT
1%
MILK
QUART (946mL)

La gente usa tazas, pintas, cuartos o galones para medir grandes cantidades de líquido.

Para cantidades más pequeñas, usa cucharitas, cucharas y onzas líquidas.

The metric system uses milliliters and liters to measure liquid. In this book, metric measurements are shown in parentheses next to the other measurements.

1 pint/pinta = 2 cups/tazas

½ pint/pinta = 1 cup/taza

1 cup/taza

El sistema métrico usa mililitros y litros para medir líquidos. En este libro, las medidas métricas se muestran entre paréntesis al lado de las otras medidas.

Now Tim can measure the water in the orange bottle with a tool.

Which tool should he pick?

The one cup tool might be too small. He picks the one that measures up to four cups.

He had 2½ cups (0.6 liter) of water in his sport bottle.

Ahora Tim puede medir el agua en la botella naranja con una herramienta.

¿Qué herramienta debería elegir?

La herramienta de una taza puede que sea muy pequeña. Él elije la que mide hasta cuatro tazas.

Él tenía 2½ tazas (0.6 litros) de agua en su botella deportiva.

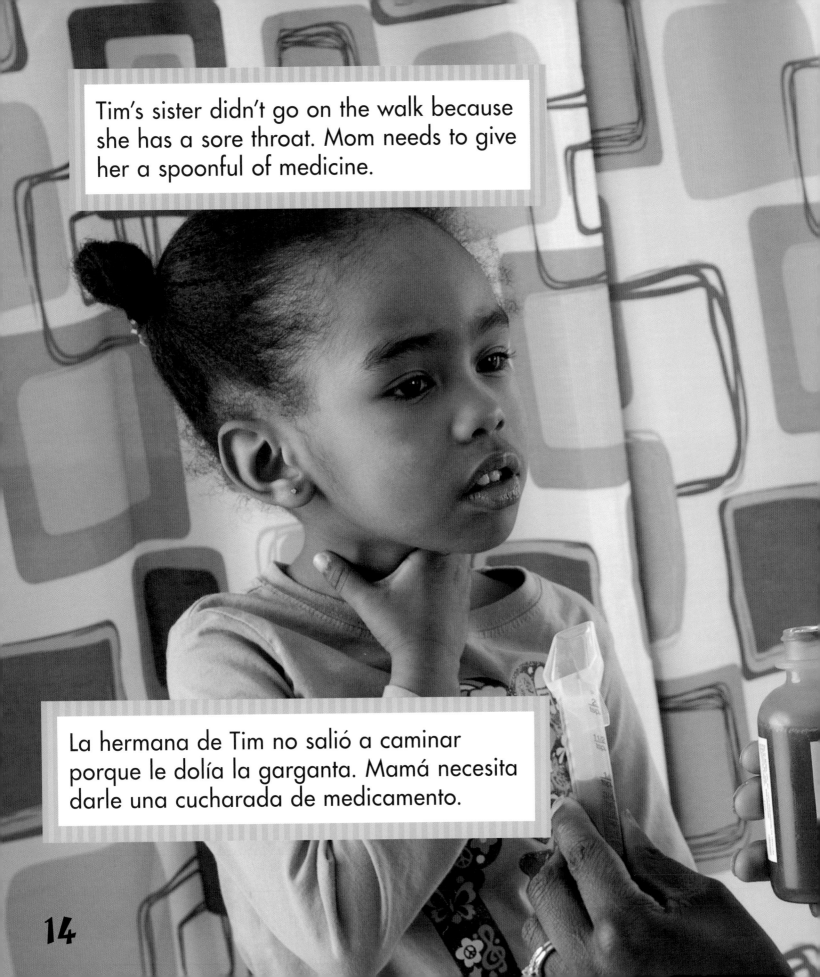

Tim's sister didn't go on the walk because she has a sore throat. Mom needs to give her a spoonful of medicine.

La hermana de Tim no salió a caminar porque le dolía la garganta. Mamá necesita darle una cucharada de medicamento.

14

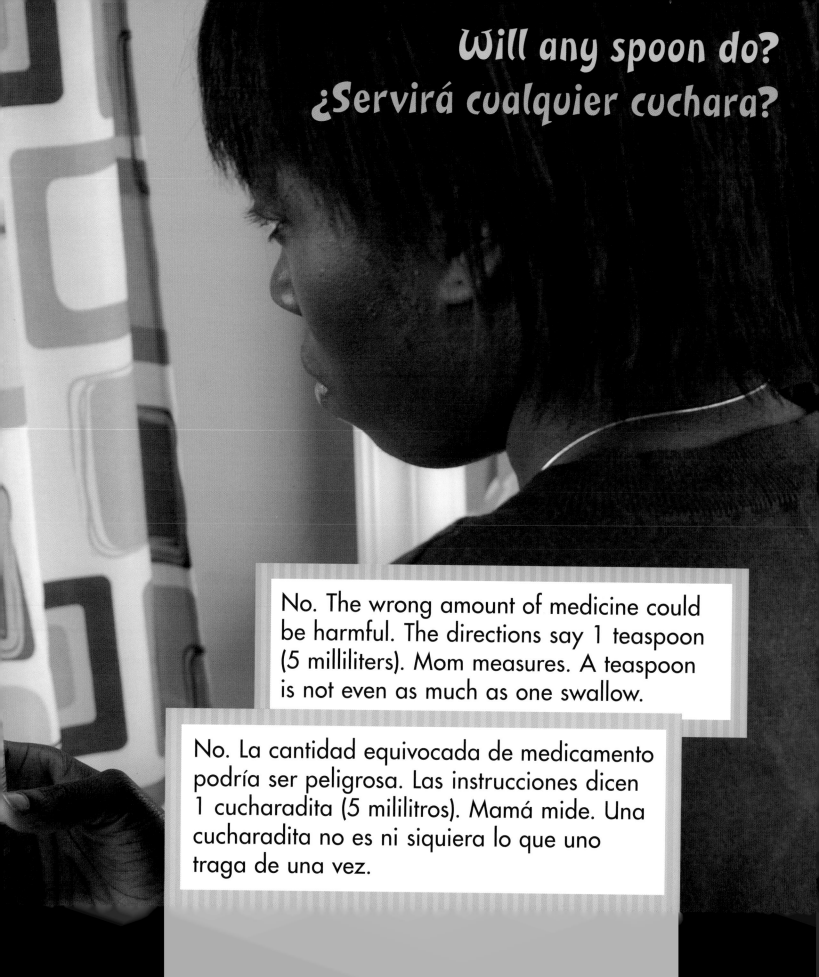

Will any spoon do?
¿Servirá cualquier cuchara?

No. The wrong amount of medicine could be harmful. The directions say 1 teaspoon (5 milliliters). Mom measures. A teaspoon is not even as much as one swallow.

No. La cantidad equivocada de medicamento podría ser peligrosa. Las instrucciones dicen 1 cucharadita (5 mililitros). Mamá mide. Una cucharadita no es ni siquiera lo que uno traga de una vez.

The next day, Tim's sister is feeling better. She and Tim can paint. Tim wants to use orange, but he has none. Mom says to mix red and yellow in equal parts.

Tim mixes ½ cup (118 mL) each of red and yellow paint. Now he's got 1 cup (237 mL) of orange!

Tim mezcla ½ taza (118 ml) de pintura roja y de pintura amarilla. ¡Ahora él tiene 1 taza (237 ml) de naranja!

16

Al día siguiente, la hermana de Tim se siente mejor. Ella y Tim pueden pintar. Tim quiere usar color naranja, pero no lo tiene. Mamá dice que mezcle cantidades iguales de rojo y amarillo.

17

Now Tim knows how to measure. He can measure the milk for hot chocolate. He needs 6 fluid ounces (177 mL) of milk.

Ahora Tim sabe cómo medir. Él puede medir la leche para el chocolate caliente. Él necesita 6 onzas líquidas (177 ml) de leche.

Tim uses the ounces marks to measure.

Tim usa las marcas de onzas para medir.

18

Delicious!
¡Delicioso!

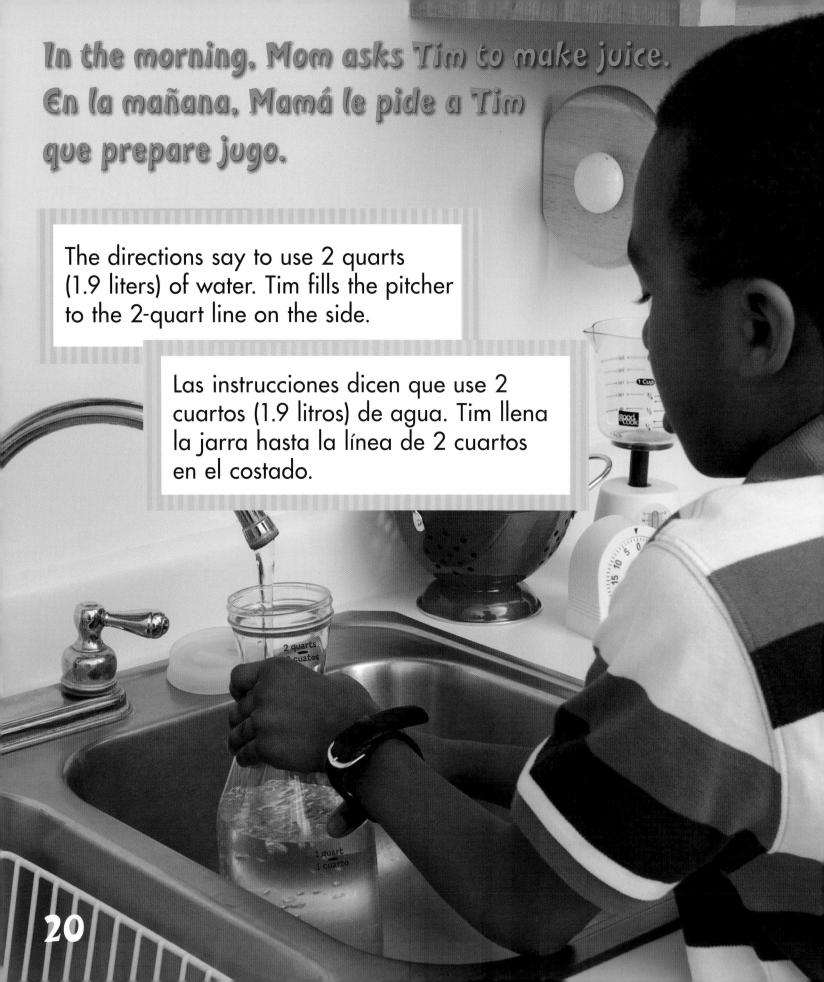

In the morning, Mom asks Tim to make juice.
En la mañana, Mamá le pide a Tim
que prepare jugo.

The directions say to use 2 quarts
(1.9 liters) of water. Tim fills the pitcher
to the 2-quart line on the side.

Las instrucciones dicen que use 2
cuartos (1.9 litros) de agua. Tim llena
la jarra hasta la línea de 2 cuartos
en el costado.

20

A quick stir, and he's done!
Revuelve rápidamente,
¡y está listo!

2 quarts
2 cuartos

1 quart
1 cuarto

21

Now it's chore time. The fish tank needs more water. How much?

Es hora de las tareas domésticas. La pecera necesita más agua. ¿Cuánta más?

1 gallon
1 galón

½ gallon
½ galón

22

Tim starts by filling up a 1-gallon (3.8-L) container of water. Then he sees how much of 1 gallon fits in the tank.

Tim comienza llenando un recipiente de 1 galón (3.8 l) con agua. Luego ve cuánto 1 galón de agua llena la pecera.

It took ½ gallon (1.9 L) of water!
¡Llevó ½ galón (1.9 l) de agua!

Tim's trying to save water. Does a shower or a bath use more water? Tim plugged the drain when he took his shower. He scooped the water into 5-gallon (19-L) pails.

Tim está tratando de ahorrar agua. ¿Qué usa más agua, una ducha o un baño? Tim tapó el drenaje cuando se duchó. Él colocó el agua en cubos de 5 galones (19 l).

Tim scooped out 3 pails. That's 15 gallons (57 L).

Tim llenó 3 cubos. Eso es 15 galones (57 l).

His sister used 20 gallons (76 L) for her bath.

Su hermana usó 20 galones (76 l) para su baño.

The shower used less water.

La ducha usó menos agua.

25

With the right tools, you can measure all kinds of liquids. Buddy got a new dog dish.

Con las herramientas correctas, tú puedes medir todo tipo de líquidos. Buddy tiene un nuevo tazón.

Who gets more
water now?

¿Quién tiene más
agua ahora?

Fun Facts about Liquid
Datos divertidos sobre líquidos

• The world's largest **fish tank** is at the Georgia Aquarium in Atlanta. It holds 6.3 million gallons (23.8 million L) of water. Two whale sharks and many other fish swim in it.

• La **pecera** más grande del mundo está en el Acuario de Georgia en Atlanta. Contiene 6.3 millones de galones de agua (23.8 millones de litros). Dos tiburones ballena y muchos otros peces nadan en el tanque.

• The average **dairy cow** produces 7 gallons (26.5 L) of milk a day.

• La **vaca lechera** común produce 7 galones (26.5 l) de leche por día.

• The **United States** uses about 380 million gallons (1.4 billion L) of gas each day.

• **Estados Unidos** usa alrededor de 380 millones de galones (1.4 mil millones de litros) de gasolina cada día.

• People use about 2 gallons (7.6 L) of water per minute during a **shower**.

• **Kids** take in about 2 quarts (1.9 L) of fluid a day, from both food and drinks. Most people get enough fluid from eating food, drinking with meals, and just drinking when they are thirsty.

• La gente usa alrededor de 2 galones (7.6 l) de agua por minuto durante una **ducha**.

• Los **niños** beben alrededor de 2 cuartos (1.9 l) de líquidos por día, tanto de alimentos como bebidas. La mayoría de la gente recibe suficientes líquidos al comer alimentos, beber con las comidas y solo beber cuando tienen sed.

Glossary

container—an object that holds something; a measuring cup is a container

cup—a unit of measure equal to 8 fluid ounces; a cup can also mean a small container for holding liquids

fluid ounce—a unit of measure for liquids that is equal to 2 tablespoons or $\frac{1}{16}$ pint

gallon—a unit of measure for liquids that is equal to 4 quarts

level—flat and even

liquid—a wet substance that can be poured

measure—to find out the size of something

metric system—a system of measurement based on counting by 10s; milliliters and liters are basic units of measuring liquid in the metric system

pint—a unit of measure equal to a half quart or 16 fluid ounces

quart—a unit of measure equal to 32 fluid ounces or 2 pints

tablespoon—a unit of measure equal to 3 teaspoons or 0.5 fluid ounce

teaspoon—a unit of measure equal to $\frac{1}{3}$ tablespoon

Internet Sites

FactHound offers a safe, fun way to find Internet sites related to this book. All of the sites on FactHound have been researched by our staff.

Here's all you do:

Visit *www.facthound.com*

Type in this code: 9781429668903

 Check out projects, games and lots more at **www.capstonekids.com**

Glosario

el cuarto—una unidad de medición equivalente a 32 onzas líquidas o 2 pintas

la cuchara—una unidad de medición equivalente a 3 cucharitas o 0.5 onzas líquidas

la cucharita—una unidad de medición equivalente a $1/3$ de cuchara

el galón—una unidad de medición para líquidos equivalente a 4 cuartos

el líquido—una sustancia mojada que puede verterse

medir—averiguar el tamaño de algo

nivelada—plana y pareja

la onza líquida—una unidad de medición para líquidos equivalente a 2 cucharas o $1/16$ pintas

la pinta—una unidad de medición equivalente a medio cuarto o 16 onzas líquidas

el recipiente—un objeto que contiene algo; una taza para medir es un recipiente

el sistema métrico—un sistema de medición basado en contar de a 10; mililitros y litros son las unidades básicas de medir líquidos del sistema métrico

la taza—una unidad de medición igual a 8 onzas líquidas; una taza también puede significar un recipiente pequeño para contener líquidos

Sitios de Internet

FactHound brinda una forma segura y divertida de encontrar sitios de Internet relacionados con este libro. Todos los sitios en FactHound han sido investigados por nuestro personal.

Esto es todo lo que tienes que hacer:

Visita *www.facthound.com*

Ingresa este código: 9781429668903

¡Algo súper divertido! Hay proyectos, juegos y mucho más en **www.capstonekids.com**

Index

Índice

A+ Books are published by Capstone Press,
1710 Roe Crest Drive, North Mankato, Minnesota 56003.
www.capstonepub.com

Library of Congress Cataloging-in-Publication Data
Adamson, Thomas K., 1970–
 [How do you measure liquids? Spanish & English]
 ¿Cómo mides los líquidos? = How do you measure liquids? /
por Thomas K. and Heather Adamson.
   p. cm.—(A+ bilingüe. Mídelo = A+ bilingual. Measure it)
 Summary: "Simple text and color photographs describe the
units and tools used to measure liquids—in both English and
Spanish"—Provided by publisher.
 Includes index.
 ISBN 978-1-4296-6890-3 (library binding)
 1. Liquids—Juvenile literature. 2. Volume (Cubic content)—
Juvenile literature. 3. Units of measurement—Juvenile literature.
I. Adamson, Heather, 1974– II. Title. III. Title: How do you
measure liquids?
QC104.A33 18 2012
530.8'1—dc22   2011001358

Credits
Gillia Olson, editor; Strictly Spanish, translation services;
 Juliette Peters, designer; Eric Manske, bilingual book designer;
 Sarah Schuette, photo studio specialist; Marcy Morin, studio
 scheduler; Laura Manthe, production specialist

Photo Credits
All photos by Capstone Studio: Karon Dubke, except:
Shutterstock: dcwcreations, 28 (bottom left), hardtmuth, 29
(top left), toroto reaction, 28 (top right)

Note to Parents, Teachers, and Librarians
The Mídelo/Measure It series uses color photographs and a
nonfiction format to introduce readers to measuring concepts in
both English and Spanish. *¿Cómo mides los líquidos?/How Do
You Measure Liquids?* is designed to be read aloud to a
pre-reader, or to be read independently by an early reader.
Images and narrative promote mathematical thinking by
showing that objects and time have measurable properties,
that comparisons such as longer or shorter can be made
between multiple objects and time-spans, and that there are
standard and non-standard units for measuring. The book
encourages further learning by including the following sections:
Fun Facts, Glossary, Internet Sites, and Index. Early readers may
need assistance using these features.

Printed in the United States of America in North Mankato, Minnesota.
082012   006803